Angora Rabbits

The Ultimate Pet Guide for Angora Rabbits

Angora Rabbit Breeding, Buying, Care, Cost, Keeping, Health, Supplies, Food, Rescue and More Included!

By Lolly Brown

Copyrights and Trademarks

All rights reserved. No part of this book may be reproduced or transformed in any form or by any means, graphic, electronic, or mechanical, including photocopying, recording, taping, or by any information storage retrieval system, without the written permission of the author.

This publication is Copyright ©2017 NRB Publishing, an imprint. Nevada. All products, graphics, publications, software and services mentioned and recommended in this publication are protected by trademarks. In such instance, all trademarks & copyright belong to the respective owners. For information consult www.NRBpublishing.com

Disclaimer and Legal Notice

This product is not legal, medical, or accounting advice and should not be interpreted in that manner. You need to do your own due-diligence to determine if the content of this product is right for you. While every attempt has been made to verify the information shared in this publication, neither the author, neither publisher, nor the affiliates assume any responsibility for errors, omissions or contrary interpretation of the subject matter herein. Any perceived slights to any specific person(s) or organization(s) are purely unintentional.

We have no control over the nature, content and availability of the web sites listed in this book. The inclusion of any web site links does not necessarily imply a recommendation or endorse the views expressed within them. We take no responsibility for, and will not be liable for, the websites being temporarily unavailable or being removed from the internet.

The accuracy and completeness of information provided herein and opinions stated herein are not guaranteed or warranted to produce any particular results, and the advice and strategies, contained herein may not be suitable for every individual. Neither the author nor the publisher shall be liable for any loss incurred as a consequence of the use and application, directly or indirectly, of any information presented in this work. This publication is designed to provide information in regard to the subject matter covered.

Neither the author nor the publisher assume any responsibility for any errors or omissions, nor do they represent or warrant that the ideas, information, actions, plans, suggestions contained in this book is in all cases accurate. It is the reader's responsibility to find advice before putting anything written in this book into practice. The information in this book is not intended to serve as legal, medical, or accounting advice.

Foreword

There are roughly 55 million Angora rabbits there and the numbers continue to rise. All of the Angora breeds produce various qualities and quantity of fiber and each has its own color. The success of selectively breeding for health and body type was again tested and gained great success. A non-molting gene in Angora rabbits has been brought out into the light.

The exact origin of this gene is unclear or whether multiple genes are responsible for the characteristics of the non-molting coat. It is partly due to these furry critters that we humans can keep and stay warm by creating some of the snuggest, warmest clothing to allow us to stave off the bitter cold.

Discover the diversity of this rabbit breed and get to know the other Angora types which currently grace lucky homes and husbandries.

Table of Contents

Introduction 1
    Glossary of Rabbit Terms 3
Chapter One: Understanding Angora Rabbits 2
    Facts about Angora Rabbits 4
    General Body Types of Rabbits 7
    Types of Angora Rabbits 9
    Angora Rabbit Standard Colors 11
    History 13
        Quick Facts 17
Chapter Two: Angora Rabbit Requirements 18
    License Requirements 19
        United States Licensing for Rabbits 20
        United Kingdom Licensing for Rabbits 22
    How Many Angora Rabbits Should You Keep? 23
    Do Angora Rabbits Get Along with Other Pets? 24
    Ease and Cost of Care 25
        Initial Costs 25
        Monthly Costs 26
    Pros and Cons of Angora Rabbits 26
Chapter Three: Purchasing Your Angora Rabbit 28
    Choosing a Reputable Angora Rabbit Breeder 29

List of Breeders and Rescue Websites 31

Selecting a Healthy Angora Rabbit 35

Chapter Four: Caring for Your Angora Rabbit 38

    Habitat Requirements for Angora Rabbits 39

        Ideal Rabbit Cage 40

        Indoor Cages vs. Outdoor Hutches 42

        Recommended Cage Accessories 43

    Litter Training Your Rabbit 44

    Handling and Taming Your Rabbit 45

Chapter Five: Meeting Your Rabbit's Nutritional Needs 46

    The Nutritional Needs of Rabbits 47

    Toxic Foods to Avoid 49

    Tips for Feeding Angora Rabbits 51

Chapter Six: Breeding Your Angora Rabbit 52

    Basic Rabbit Breeding Information 54

    Mating Behavior of Rabbits 56

    Nesting Requirements 57

    Diet and Labor Process for Pregnant Angora Rabbits 58

    Raising Baby Rabbits 60

Chapter Seven: Grooming Your Angora Rabbit 64

    Recommended Tools to Have on Hand 65

    Tips for Bathing and Grooming Angora Rabbits 67

Other Grooming Tasks 70
Chapter Eight: Showing Angora Rabbits 72
  Angora Rabbit Breed Standards 73
    Preparing Your Rabbit for Show 78
Chapter Nine: Keeping Your Rabbit Healthy 82
  Common Health Problems Affecting Rabbits 83
  Preventing Illness 85
  Recommended Vaccinations 86
  Signs of Possible Illnesses 87
Rabbit Care Sheet 88
  Basic Information 89
  Habitat Requirements 90
  Nutritional Needs 91
  Breeding Information 93
Index 96
Photo Credits 102
References 104

Introduction

This soft, fluffy cottontail which originated from Turkey is a domesticated rabbit and is bred for its soft, long wool. This specie of rabbit is one of the oldest sorts of domestic rabbit which hails from Ankara, historically known as Angora, Turkey. It shares nationality with the Angora goat and Angora cat.

These rabbits were sought after pets of French royalty in the mid-18th century and proliferated to other parts of the European continent by the end of the 20th century.

Introduction

These furry rabbits first made their presence known in the United States sometime during the early 20th century. The adorable fur-balls are largely bred for their soft and long Angora wool which is collected by shearing, plucking or combing.

Angora rabbits come in a myriad of individual breeds. Four of the Angora breeds are currently recognized by the American Rabbit Breeders Association (ARBA). Find out more about these breeds of rabbit, sought after due to their intelligent, docile, friendly and adorably fuzzy bunny, as you read on further.

Should you be looking to care for one, or a few, of these generally docile animals as pet or to harvest Angora wool, you will find useful tips, information and bits that will aid in your quest. Read on to discover what needs to be known about the Angora rabbit; its nutrition, health, breeding methods, habitat and how to generally care for this adorably, soft creature.

Introduction

Glossary of Rabbit Terms

Agouti – A type of coloring in which the hair shaft has three or more bands of color with a definite break between.

Albino – A pink-eyed, white-furred rabbit.

Alter - To remove the sex organs of a rabbit. To be "fixed" or spayed (female term) or neutered (male term).

ARBA – The American Rabbit Breeders Association; an organization which promotes rabbits in the United States.

Arch (Arc) - Rabbit term to describe a gentle curvature of the spine, which extends from the neck (or shoulders in some breeds) to the rear of the rabbit. It is best observed by viewing the animal in profile.

Awn – The strong, straight guard hairs protruding above the undercoat in angora breeds.

Balance – An orderly and pleasing arrangement of physical characteristics promoting a harmonious appearance.

Base Color – The color of the fur next to the skin.

Bangs - The longer wool appearing at the front base of the ears and top of the head in some wooled breeds.

Bare Spot - A portion of the rabbit's pelt that lacks fur due to molt or any other cause.

Barn - Similar to rabbitry. People refer to their rabbit barn as such if they keep their rabbits in their own unique building just for the purpose of housing rabbits.

Introduction

Bell Ears – Ears that have large tips with distinct similar to a giant rabbit breeds.

Belly - The lower part of the body containing the intestines, the abdomen. For purposes of defining color area, it is the underbody of the rabbit from the forelegs to the crotch area.

Belly Color - The color on the underside of the rabbit, extending from the forelegs to the crotch area

Belt – The line where the colored portion of the coat meets the white portion, just behind the shoulders.

Binky or Binkies - This is when a rabbit is extremely happy and jumps into the air while running or while standing still. Sometimes they will kick out their hind legs in midair too. Domestic rabbits as well as wild rabbits will do this. It's a wonderful sight to see.

Blaze – A white marking found on the head of the Dutch rabbit; the shape is wedge-like.

Bloom - The vitality and finish of a coat in good condition.

BOB - A rabbit term used in show circles, a show award meaning Best of Breed; denotes the best of a particular breed that day.

Bonding – A rabbit term used to describe two rabbits that have paired up together. The easiest bond is male to female but female to female and male to male bonds are also possible. Once rabbits are bonded they shouldn't really be separated or it will put undue stress on the rabbits.

Cecotrope Pellet - This is the rabbit poop that is normally eaten right from the anus directly. It is mulberry/brownish in

Introduction

color, shaped like a small raspberry with white-ish mucus covering it. It can look like a cluster of tiny, shiny poops all clumped and stuck together. For nutritional reasons, rabbits re-ingest these pellets.

Cecotrophy - Consumption of the cecal pellets that are swallowed whole without chewing directly from the anus. They are dependent on the rabbit eating a lot of fiber to product them.

Cecum - Largest part of the GI tract of a rabbit. Has 10 times the capacity of its stomach. Contains 40% of the intestinal content and is the fermentation vat where food gets processed.

Dew Claw - An extra toe or functionless digit on the inside of the front leg.

Dewlap - A pendulous fold of loose skin which hangs from the throat. When the rabbit is altered (fixed) the dewlap will normally disappear. It should be in proportion to the total body size, not accepted in some breeds. Disqualification or DQ One or more permanent defects, deformities, or blemishes that make a rabbit unfit to win an award in competition or to take part in an exhibition.

Doe – An unaltered female rabbit.

Flat Coat – Fur lying too close to the body, lacking spring and body as noted by touch.

DQ - Disqualification from showing. DQ's may be either permanent (such as a missing toe, malocclusion, or

Introduction

nonshowable colour) or temporary (illness). Most common is over the weight limit, bad teeth, or illness present.

Ear Canker - An inflamed scabby condition deep inside the ear. It is caused by an infestation of the ear canal by rabbit ear mites.

Ear Lacing - A colored line of fur which outlines the sides and tips of the ears.

Ear Number / Tattoo - A series of numbers and/or letters tattooed into the rabbits left ear. Usually no more than 5 are in the ear. A circled R may be tattooed in the left ear if the rabbit has been registered.

Elimination - One or more defects presumed to be temporary and curable. Cause for elimination in a show or from registration until cured or corrected.

Embryo - A kit in the early stages of development inside the doe.

Enteritis (or diarrhea) - Inflammation of the intestinal tract which can often be a fatal illness of the digestive system characterized by diarrhea and brought on by stress, excessive carbohydrate consumption and/or weaning. Rabbit's poop pellets should be firm and dry looking and slightly smaller than marbles.

Entry - Entries are rabbits that will participate in a particular show.

Flabby - The condition of a rabbit when the flesh or fur hangs loosely. Not trim and shapely.

Introduction

Flank - The sides of the rabbit between the ribs and hips and above the belly.

Flat Coat - Fur lying too closely to the body. Lacks spring or body as noted by touch. Usually a fine coat coupled with a lack of density.

Flat Shoulders - A trait that occurs when the top line over the shoulders is noticeably parallel to the surface of the judging table. A lack of continuous arch from the neck over the shoulders.

Flesh Condition - The general health and state of a rabbit's skin. If a rabbit is "rough" in flesh it means the skin over the backbone is very loose and thin. Bones are easily felt.

Fryer – A young meat rabbit no more than 10 weeks of age and weighing less than 5 pounds.

Gestation – The period of time between breeding and birthing (or kindling).

Guard Hair – The long, coarser hairs in a rabbit's coat which protect the undercoat.

Herd – A group of rabbits.

Inbreeding – Breeding of closely related stock.

Junior – A class of rabbits referring to those under 6 months of age.

Kindling – The process of giving birth to baby rabbits (kits).

Kindling Box – A box provided for a pregnant rabbit so she can make a nest and give birth.

Kit – A baby rabbit.

Introduction

Line Breeding – A breeding program in which rabbits that are descended from the same animal are bred.

Litter – A group of young rabbits born to one doe at the same time.

Loose Coat – A condition of fur lacking density in the undercoat, often coupled with fine guard hairs resulting in a lack of texture.

Malocclusion – A misalignment of the rabbit's teeth.

Molt – The process of shedding or changing the fur, happens twice each year.

Nest Box – A box provided for a pregnant rabbit so she can make a nest and give birth.

Nursing – The process of kits suckling milk from the dam's teats; usually occurs twice a day.

Peanut – A rabbit with two dwarf genes; usually fatal.

Pelage – The fur coat or covering in a rabbit.

Pellets – May refer either to the rabbit's poop or its food.

Quick – The pink part of the nails/claws that contains the blood vessels and nerves.

Racy – Referring to a slim, slender body and legs.

Saddle – The rounded portion of the back between the rabbit's shoulder and loin.

Self-Colored – A fur pattern where the hair colors are the same all over the body.

Sire – A male rabbit that has produced offspring.

Thumping – The practice of banging or stomping the hind legs on the ground to make a loud, thudding noise.

Introduction

Ticking - A wavy distribution of longer guard hairs throughout the rabbit's coat.

Weaning – The process in which baby rabbits become independent of their dam, transitioning to solid food.

Wool – A term used to describe the fur of Angora rabbits.

Introduction

Chapter One: Understanding Angora Rabbits

Amongst all the rabbit breeds worldwide, and there are indeed plenty of them, the Angora breeds are the rabbits most outstanding. It is distinctively different from other rabbit breeds due to their gorgeously flowing, soft and supple wool. It is to be noted that Angora rabbits are prized by both rabbit enthusiasts and fiber artists because of their characteristic fur that has been sought after the world over since the discovery of its utilitarian uses. Discover more facts about these stands out rabbits and learn a little more about their varied appearances, traits and qualities.

Chapter One: Understanding Angora Rabbits

There are presently four breeds of Angora rabbits which are recognized by the American Rabbit Breeders Association. Meet the Giant Angora, the Satin Angora, the French Angora and the English Angora within these pages and see which one of them captures your heart the most.

These four breeds mentioned above are the ones which pop into mind when people mention and think of Angora rabbits. This is partly because of their easy-to-recall names and their sizes. You will also learn a little about the Jersey Wooly and the American Fuzzy Lop, which are the other types of Angoras, who are notably smaller in size; these smaller Angoras (not recognized by the ARBA) do possess the angora wool - which make them uniquely Angoras - however, it would take a lot more rabbits to gain the same amount of wool one can garner it from one of the other larger Angora breeds.

The Angora is a breed of rabbit which requires lots of grooming and requires it daily. These long-furred bunnies need to be given a good brushing every day to prevent the matting of its thick wool.

The French Angora's fur is coarser than the other Angoras fur and has more guard hair than others, so their coats are easier to groom. On the contrary, the English

Chapter One: Understanding Angora Rabbits

Angora requires daily grooming to maintain the described breed standard of its roundish-ball-of-fur appearance.

Potential Angora rabbit breeders will be glad to learn that harvesting angora wool is quite an easy process IF one knows what they are doing. Angora wool is usually harvested by shearing or plucking; however, the specifics of harvesting do depend on the situation and the breed. A novice guardian should seek the help of a seasoned rabbit breeder in order to find out the best and safest method of harvesting the Angora's wool. Let's put the spotlight on the biggest and smallest of the Angora breeds.

Facts about Angora Rabbits

Aptly named, the Giant Angora is the largest of the Angora breeds typically weighing in around 9.5-10 pounds when mature. The smallest of the Angora breed is the Jersey Wooly weighing in at less than 3.5 pounds.

There is no other Angora breed which combines the flowing softness and translucence of Angora fur than that of the Satin Angora. Whilst these Angoras typically do not produce as much wool which can be harvested like the other big Angoras, the wool of the Satin Angora is unique for its

Chapter One: Understanding Angora Rabbits

satiny qualities, making them more appealing to Angora enthusiasts.

The origins of Angora rabbits are unclear. However, these large, furry rabbits have been documented in the distant past and mention of them dates back to the eighteenth century. The Angoras of present day supposedly descended from a sort of Turkish rabbit bred for its very fine wool. It is said that sailors of yore recognized the value of these rabbits so they acquired some to take back to their home country, France. It was in France where the breed was said to be mentioned in a 1765 encyclopedia. After which it became a sought after pet amongst French aristocracy.

Many Angora Clubs have been founded and are committed to the care and advancement of Angora rabbits. The National Angora Rabbit Breeders Club, Inc. is "dedicated to the promotion and care of Angora rabbits" and is the national club for the four larger Angora breeds. The American Fuzzy Lop and the Jersey Wooly have established their own respective clubs which are the American Fuzzy Lop Rabbit Club and the National Jersey Wooly Rabbit Club.

It was the first half of the nineteenth century when the first Angora rabbits landed in the United States. Back then all Angora rabbits were categorized together as one

Chapter One: Understanding Angora Rabbits

breed; the Angora Wooler. It was in 1939 when this changed and when ARBA started separating the Angoras into the French type and English type rabbits. These rabbits finally became distance and separate breeds in 1944. It was then they became known as the names they are called today. It was in 1987 when the ARBA approved the Satin Angora and was followed by the Giant Angora in 1988.

The English Angora, French Angora and Satin Angora breeds come in an assortment of rainbow colors recognized by the ARBA. These rabbits are allowed to be shown. The color assortment include Ruby-Eyed White, Blue-Eyed White, Tortoiseshell, Seal, Sable, Red, Pointed White, Opal, Lynx, Lilac, Fawn, Copper, Chocolate, Chinchilla, Chestnut, Blue, and Black.

In addition, Satin and French Angoras can also be Siamese Smoke Pearl. It is only the French Angora which exhibits the broken color pattern. The Giant Angora is only recognized by the ARBA in one color and that is Ruby-Eyed White. If the color is not a Ruby-Eyed White then it is not considered an Angora.

Chapter One: Understanding Angora Rabbits

General Body Types of Rabbits

Like other living beings, rabbits also come in different shapes and forms. Find out about the various types of rabbit physique and their sizes here.

Full Arch

The full-arch breed is the ones which are always naturally alert and energetic. Rabbits of this body type have an arch which begins at the nape of the neck and continues in a fluid, unbroken line over the rabbit's shoulders, loin, hips and ends by rounding to the base of its tail. Most breeds will display more depth than body width. Its side profile tapers from the hind quarters through to the rabbits shoulders. Many of these full-arch sorts have notably erect ears and have a spotted fur coat.

Some full-arched breeds are the Britannia Petite, Checkered Giant, the English Spot, the Belgian Hare, the Tan and the Rhinelander.

Semi-Arch

Semi-Arch rabbits are usually referred to as "Gentle Giants" due to their larger size. These rabbits have low shoulders with a high hip. The rabbit's side profile is tapered from the hindquarters through to its shoulders.

Chapter One: Understanding Angora Rabbits

Some notable semi-arch breeds are the Giant Chinchilla, the Flemish Giant, the English Lop, the Beveren and the American.

Compact

Some smaller breeds of rabbits constitute the category of Compact rabbit breeds. These rabbits are lighter in weight and shorter in body length compared to the commercial type of rabbits. Some breeds sport a slight rise in the top line because of the depth of its shoulders is slightly lower than the depth over its hips. When viewed from its side profile, it is tapered or has equal width from hips to shoulders, as required in the individual breed standard. Compact rabbits will appear well balanced when properly set up.

Some Compact breeds are the Thrianta, the Standard Chinchilla, the Silver, the Polish, the Netherland Dwarf, the Mini Satin, the Mini Rex, the Mini Lop, the Lilac, the Jersey Wooly, the Holland Lop, the Havana, the Florida White, the English Angora, the Dwarf Hotot, the Dutch, and the American Fuzzy Lop.

Commercial

Commercial rabbit breeds are usually used as meat rabbits and production animals. These rabbits tend to grow faster and large meaty loins. These rabbit sorts are medium in length with a depth of body equal to the width of its body throughout. The high point of the top line is to be over the rabbits hips. Its side profile tapers from the hindquarters all the way through to its shoulders. Commercial rabbits look very similar to the "Compact Rabbit Breeds" only they are much bigger than the compact ones.

Some Commercial Breeds include the Silver Marten, the Silver Fox, the Satin Angora, the Satin, the Rex, the Palomino, the New Zealand, the Harlequin, the Giant Angora, the French Lop, the French Angora, the Creme d' Argent, the Cinnamon, the Champagne d' Argent, the Californian, the Blanc de Hotot, the American Sable, and the American Chinchilla.

Cylindrical

The rabbit breed known as the Cylindrical sort currently has one member in the Himalayan. Himalayan rabbits look a lot like the Californian, only much smaller. They do, however, share the same cylindrical shape in nature.

Types of Angora Rabbits

Aside from the Angora rabbit, there are many other individual breeds of these Angora cottontails. Other breeds

Chapter One: Understanding Angora Rabbits

of this sort are the Giant Angora, the Satin Angora, the English Angora and the French Angora.

All Angora rabbits have a special diet requirement and they need daily attention in terms of grooming. A dedicated caregiver/keeper of one has their mind set on making the grooming process of the Angora part of their daily routine.

The Giant Angora weighs around 12 pounds, with females weighing heavier. It sports a commercial body with a large oval head which is broad on the forehead, slightly narrowing at the muzzle. These rabbits have facial forehead tufts and cheek furnishings. Its ears are well tasseled and lightly fringed.

The English Angora weighs around 5-7 pounds and its thick wool covers the rabbits' entire body, including its face and its stand-up ears. This gives the English Angora the appearance of a big fur ball and they come in many colors.

The French Angora weighs around 7 1/2-10 1/2 pounds and sport medium-sized, long rounded bodies with long, erect ears. Its face, ears, and fore feet have short fur and the rest of its body sports very long, soft wool. They come in different colors through breeding. As with all Angoras, the French Angora needs a special diet and needs to be carefully groomed every day to avoid molting.

Chapter One: Understanding Angora Rabbits

The other breeds of Angora include the Swiss, Finnish, Chinese, German, Korean and St. Lucian Angora.

Angora Rabbit Standard Colors

The American Rabbit Breeders Association presently recognizes four of the Angora breeds in its registry. These breeds are the English Angora, the French Angora, the Satin Angora and the Giant Angora. The Angora is sought after not only as a family pet to enjoy days with, it is also in demand for its thick, woolen coat.

Before 1939, Angoras were classified as one breed - the Angora Wooler. It was in this year when ARBA classified the Angora Wooler into two types; the English type and the French type. Only in 1944 did ARBA separate the two Angora types into two breeds; the English Angora and the French Angora. Due to the Angoras popularity many Rabbit Clubs have been founded by rabbit aficionados purposely for the advancement, promotion and care of these generally docile creatures.

Each of the Angora rabbit breeds come in a variety of colors. Let's find out what color varieties are acceptable to ARBA. The American Rabbit Breeders Association

Chapter One: Understanding Angora Rabbits

recognizes the four Angora breeds and is very straight forward with color requirements for these Angoras.

The smallest and gentlest of the breed, the English Angora rabbit, requires regular combing and grooming because of its very dense wool. Those who have an already full schedule should rethink acquiring one because the rabbit cannot be left to neglect. The only rabbit breed which has fur covering and hiding its eyes, the English Angora is a sweet ball of fur that is easy to fall in love with. ARBA accepts English Angoras in varieties of agouti, self-shaded, broken, pointed white and ruby-eyed white.

The French Angora is much larger than its English cousin and it sports a commercial body type with a big undercoat. It differs from the other Angoras because it has a hairless face and forelegs that is save for minor tufting on its rear legs. Its wool fiber is of a smooth silky texture. The ARBA accepted French Angora varieties are self, agouti, ticked, pointed white, shaded, brown tones, broken, and white band.

The largest of all Angoras and the one which produces the most wool amongst the four breeds is the Giant Angora. The Giant Angora, which has a commercial body type and possesses a very dense coat of wool, mostly

Chapter One: Understanding Angora Rabbits

appears in ruby-eyed white and this is the only color accepted by the ARBA.

The result of cross breeding between a French Angora rabbit and a Satin is the Satin Angora. Not a big producer of wool as its other Angora cousins, the Satin Angoras wool is silky in texture, has high luster with good guard hair. Shaded, agouti, self, wide band and pointed white are the varieties accepted by ARBA.

These lovably, fluffy, friendly, docile rabbits are typically raised as pets and more often kept and cared for because of their production of fine quality wool.

History

The beginning of the Angora Rabbits history dates back in the times of the Romans. It was surmised that Romans raised, bred and used Angora rabbit wool as far back as 100 BC. As best as can be determined, this breed of rabbit was established in Eastern Europe sometime around 500 - 600 AD and was perhaps brought there by the Romans.

The Carpathian Mountains of Transylvania, between Hungary and Romania) experienced harsh winters and

Chapter One: Understanding Angora Rabbits

bone-numbing cold weather. The tribes who resided there raised herds of captive Angoras to breed them for the warm wool they provided.

These tribes also raised goats for the mohair fibers they provided, but preferred the Angora wool when possible because of its soft texture and it was lightweight but warm.

For over a millennium, the Angora rabbit was called Angola up until the 1800s. Angola was a word that Romanian tribes used to describe the wool of the rabbit. Angola loosely meant "un-scratchy".

In the 1500s the history of the Angora rabbit picks up trail in England, where English law made the export of the "English Silk Hare" - once the name of the Angora rabbit in England then. These restrictions were to last 200 years.

England was a dominant world power to reckon with and reigned supremacy on the open seas. Merchant ships from England sailed far and wide throughout the known world. It wouldn't be a stretch to assume that there could have been a regular smuggling of these rabbits out of the country and sold to distant shores where the rabbits would not be discovered.

Chapter One: Understanding Angora Rabbits

It was in 1723 when the first angoras arrived in the south of France in the city of Bordeaux. English seafarers who brought them along on their ocean voyages sold them for exorbitant prices.

The French Encyclopedia of Sciences is firm in maintaining that Angoras got their beginnings in Europe, namely France, in 1765. This documented information contradicts the occurrence of the rabbits in the country as early as 1723. It is possible that the wool industry officially began on this given year, hence the oversight.

Not long after, Angoras which had begun to populate Germany came from England sometime in 1777, when Herr von Meyersbach imported them to the country.

Father Charles Mayer, a priest, was vital and instrumental in the spread of Angoras throughout Germany. He also taught farmers how to best care for both the rabbit as well as its wool.

Around 1780 – 1781, the Prussian government sponsored prizes for the exceptional wool production of Angora. Angoras were a royal pet favorite in France. Marie Antoinette, the Queen of France, kept Angora rabbits for pets in the palace. Both the queen and her rabbits met the

Chapter One: Understanding Angora Rabbits

same fate on October 5, 1789 - when the queen was executed and her rabbits brutally destroyed.

The Emperor of France, Napoleon, held great fascination for the furry Angoras and was said to have clandestinely commissioned machines that could spin wool in large volumes. These spinning machines were later discovered after World War II.

There is factual evidence of the presence of Angoras in the shores of the United States as early as 1840. During that period of time the luxuriously fluffy rabbits were still called Angolas. Those who saw the advantages and promise of the ultra-lightweight yet exceedingly warm angora wool paved the way for a new industry. Hardworking individuals were now able to earn a living for themselves. Whilst those enterprising enough and were of means were able to create jobs to employ an entire neighborhood.

France was the primary provider of raw wool production until late 1965. China currently produces 95% of the wool supply globally. Owing to the educational resources given by Father Mayer, breeders have been improving the growth and output of wool by castrating bucks.

Chapter One: Understanding Angora Rabbits

Angoras photographed prior to 1880 display an angora with short, smooth fur from head to toe. Presently, French angoras more closely appear like the angora as it appeared through time, but perhaps with more extravagant fur owing to years of selective breeding.

Quick Facts

This furry, fluffy, usually friendly bunny rabbit is one of the oldest rabbits of the domestic variety. It originated from Angora - presently known as Ankara - Turkey. The Angora rabbit was, and still is, mainly bred for its soft, supple, luscious, long wool.

In the mid-18th century, Angora rabbits were a hit and widely sought after as pets amongst French royalty. By the end of the century its kind eventually spread out and reached other parts of Europe.

It was in the early parts of the 20th century when the Angora rabbit initially made its presence known in the United States and where this breed of rabbit was bred for its lengthy Angora wool. Its dense wool grows pretty rapidly and needs to be harvested every 3-4 months, depending on size and length of coat. Its wool is harvested by plucking, shearing or combing.

Chapter Two: Angora Rabbit Requirements

The wool of the Angora is a fiber of luxury with many special qualities. It is soft, lustrous and seven times warmer than that of sheep's wool. These fibers possess an inner structure which provides Angora garments and yarns a thermal quality.

This chapter aims to reveal requirements a keeper would need to satisfy in order to successfully raise a well-rounded, healthy Angora rabbit.

Chapter Two: Angora Rabbit Requirements

License Requirements

Determining license requirements for the Angora rabbit is a question frequently asked by novice keepers. They want to know how many rabbits they can keep and if a certain number of acquired rabbits deem obtaining a license.

The Angora rabbit is a wool fiber producing animal and its wool is widely sought after by hobbyists. Should a caregiver of an Angora rabbit wish to turn their hobby into a side business and start profiting off of the rabbits wool, they will simply need a business plan and a booth at their local Farmer's Market.

In New South Wales keeping two domestic type rabbits was made legal in October 1995. This opened the way for commercial rabbit farming there.

It is illegal to keep a wild rabbit as a pet or for commercial purposes in NSW as wild rabbits have been carrier of and has spread Rabbit Calicivirus Disease (RCD) across many parts of Australia radically reducing the European wild rabbit population in some locales.

Chapter Two: Angora Rabbit Requirements

Guidelines have been set in these places in order for individuals to be able to raise rabbits for meat or fiber-producing business.

United States Licensing for Rabbits

Owning an Angora rabbit as a pet does not require a license in the United States. Private breeders breed their Angoras with the intent of selling the rabbits for profit to interested buyers. Those wishing to register their Angora should apply with rabbit clubs and associations directly. Registry with a rabbit club does not necessitate showing your Angora.

The need and acquisition of a rabbit license will largely depend on why a license is needed. A rabbit license will be required for those looking to venture into the business of supplying rabbits for research purposes.

Rabbit dealers and breeders making anywhere from $600 - $1000 are required to obtain a USDA breeders license. Commercial producers of pets which sell to brokers, pet stores and wholesalers are all licensed according to the AWA.

Chapter Two: Angora Rabbit Requirements

If a keeper wishes to venture into supplying lab rabbits (not Angoras, mind you) they would then most certainly need to obtain a license to operate a business of this scale.

All research facilities are mandated by the AWA to care for the animals in a humane manner. To maintain standards, research and lab facilities utilizing animals are licensed and inspected by the USDA.

Small, part-time farms of agricultural producers in Pennsylvania operate under Pennsylvania's Clean Stream Law. One specific portion of this law is the Nutrient Management Act. All farms are a potential source of groundwater or surface pollution.

Portions of this law may apply to you depending on the mix of enterprises you may have or want to establish. If a keeper intends to keep a large number of pets in a rabbit farm, they should get in touch with their city's Soil and Water Conservation District to find out which of the regulations apply to the intended operation.

It would be wise to pay your local municipal hall a visit where you can inquire about state regulations regarding the ownership of Angora rabbits which may apply to you.

Chapter Two: Angora Rabbit Requirements

United Kingdom Licensing for Rabbits

The Rural Lands Protection Act 1989, of New South Wales, presently requires every individual who wishes to keep two or more rabbits to apply for and obtain a license.

The Act calls for rabbits to be vaccinated with the fibroma vaccine. A licensing kit which contains an application form and relevant literature on the conditions of keeping rabbits can be obtained through the NSW Agriculture offices.

Rabbits are to be kept in adherence to the Model Code of Practice for the Welfare of Animals - Intensive Husbandry of Rabbits. This is a needed requirement to obtain a license. The Code gives specifics on cage sizes as well as food and water provisions to farmed rabbits. It likewise stipulates methods for the proper handling and transport of the rabbits.

Pet rabbits should in no way be, or come from the, wild. Instead the pet rabbit should be a recognized domestic breed or hybrid of a domestic bred. It should be kept in a rabbit-proof enclosure. Rabbits are not to be released, left alone or abandoned.

Chapter Two: Angora Rabbit Requirements

Should an inspector pay a visit to a rabbit husbandry, the keeper is obliged to allow for an ocular inspection of the premises where the rabbits reside.

Kept rabbits are not to be vaccinated with the fibroma vaccine nor should it be kept in or brought into the premises. Rabbits which have been vaccinated with the fibroma vaccine cannot be kept or brought onto the premises.

All rabbits are to be kept in accordance with the Code of Practice for Intensive Husbandry of Rabbits, produced by the Animal Health Committee to the Standing Committee on Agriculture and Resource Management.

How Many Angora Rabbits Should You Keep?

Angora rabbits are staunchly territorial, and in many cases, when they are kept together in one enclosure, they will end up fighting at some point. This is not true for this rabbit breed that prefers the silence and its own company. If you are the keeper provide care and attention to your rabbit on a daily basis.

There were, however; reported cases of multiple rabbits which were successfully kept together in an enclosure without fighting. Should you wish to have more than one rabbit share the same space, it is strongly recommended to introduce them to each other at a young age - in order for them to get used to each other, grow together and discover things as a pair. Keep a sharp eye out and watch for aggressive behavior. If this should happen, be ready to separate them hurriedly so as to prevent injury to any of the animals.

Do Angora Rabbits Get Along with Other Pets?

Rabbits are generally social creatures with gentle natures and signature personalities needing just as much of your attention as a cat or dog would seek it.

Adults often make the well-meaning but misguided mistake of acquiring rabbits to gift children. This is a major no-no as rabbits are not suitable pets for children. Rabbits require, almost demand, specific foods, environment which stimulate its faculties and specialized vet care who are learned, aware and up to date of the ins and outs of rabbit health care.

If, and this is a big IF, existing pets like a cat or dog (or both) have been properly socialized and has experienced and been exposed to other animals without incident, then the rabbit should be safe and chances are high that they will all get along fine. Make sure that an adult caregiver is present for the initial meeting and can mediate the situation should it get intense.

Ease and Cost of Care

Angora rabbits need a specialized sort of care, whether they are kept as pets or as wool producers. As pets they require a decent amount of your time to help them groom their fur, get nourishment, exercise and affection. The following chapters will reveal the monetary amount of acquisition to expenses related to daily, monthly and annual care.

The most important thing to determine when considering taking in an Angora is your commitment and dedication to its welfare and daily care.

Initial Costs

Whilst a collective number of breeders state that high-quality, healthy Angoras of breeding stock can be obtained for as little as $50, there are breeders who would sell these rabbits in excess of $200. Show rabbits are costlier than rabbits acquires for other uses.

Chapter Two: Angora Rabbit Requirements

There is a market for high-quality show rabbits. However, rabbits of show stock may not be suitable for breeding purposes. Keep this in mind when considering breeding your show rabbit.

The American Pet Products Association has suggested that pet owners dole out around $116 every year on their pet rabbits. It would be safe to assume that owners of show rabbits spend a little more than this amount for their high-quality show pet.

Monthly Costs

Your Angora rabbit will need to replenish its food supplies each month along with a couple of other necessities like non-surgical veterinary care. According to the APPA, the average yearly cost of caring and providing for the needs of an Angora rabbit can cost an average of $116 a year.

Pros and Cons of Angora Rabbits

There are many upsides to taking in an Angora rabbit as a pet. Not only is it a friendly, docile, intelligent animal to have as a family pet, its wooly fur is highly sought after as well by crafters and hobbyists.

Chapter Two: Angora Rabbit Requirements

A keeper can make some extra money on the side with the wool of their Angora and sell it directly to interested buyers. Rabbit manure is another lucrative money maker because it is makes for excellent fertilizer and can be sold to gardeners and farmers in the area.

Any individual hoping to make a profit out of their hobby has to first figure out what sort of small business they will be willing to undertake because there will be some sort of investment- in the form of time, money and effort - to be allotted. An individual looking to care for an Angora should be ready for the daily routine of grooming the animal as its dense fur, if left un-groomed, will tend to molt and tangle.

Chapter Three: Purchasing Your Angora Rabbit

So, you may be closer to making a decision on whether or not the Angora rabbit would be suitable for you and your family to take in as pet. This is an opportune time to ask yourself once again if the Angora is the right pet for you to bring home, if its traits jive with yours and if you can provide for and meet its needs.

As you inch closer to making a decision it is also the perfect time to crunch numbers to determine if the household income will be able to sustain not only the nutrition of the Angora but also its basic daily requirements.

Chapter Three: Purchasing Your Angora Rabbit

Figuring out the initial costs at this time allows a potential Angora guardian to prepare all that the Angora would need in terms of enclosure, nutrition, toys, grooming tools, sundries, etc.

This adorable looking creature, usually covered from head to toe in dense wool, is widely available in the country if one knows how and where to look.

Your next assignment, in this quest of yours to have an Angora (or two) join the ranks of your family, is to search for a reputable breeder you can trust - a breeder with a history of breeding success who will hand over a healthy Angora rabbit.

Choosing a Reputable Angora Rabbit Breeder

As you get closer to making your decision about taking in an Angora rabbit, the important task of finding a reputable breeder is on the table.

If you are looking for breeders who are in this business out of love and personal gratification whilst making a wee bit of a profit can be hard to come across.

Chapter Three: Purchasing Your Angora Rabbit

You don't want to purchase from "fly-by-night" breeders whose sole goal is to make a quick buck run a-plenty. It will be up to you to sift and weed out the undesirables to get to the upstanding breeders to consider.

Breeders of upstanding repute will be willing and open to disclosing the rabbit's history to a potential caregiver. They will be happy to share information about the rabbit and would remember to mention milestones in the rabbit's life.

In turn, be prepared to answer a few questions from the breeder. A good breeder who has the future well-being of the rabbit in mind will also want to find out about the home the bunny may eventually join. Many successful breeders have refused to part with an animal due to the shady future ahead of the critter in the hands of a buyer who doesn't possess the qualities of a responsible caregiver.

The Angora rabbit requires special attention and care, so the breeder may ask you if you will be available to meet its needs and groom the rabbit regularly. They may also inquire about the presence of another responsible adult/caregiver in the event of your absence. They may ask if you have existing pets at home and what sort they are. They will be ready to give you tips on how to set up its enclosure.

Chapter Three: Purchasing Your Angora Rabbit

List of Breeders and Rescue Websites

There are so many Angora rabbit breeds to choose from, that's why you need to do some research and decide which breed you want before you start shopping around. When you are ready to buy a rabbit, you then need to start thinking about where you are going to get it. You may be able to find an Angora rabbit at your local pet store, but think carefully before you buy whether that is really the best option. When you buy a rabbit from a pet store you have no way of knowing where the rabbit came from – you also don't know anything about the quality of its breeding.

If you want a baby rabbit, your best chance is to find a local rabbit breeder. Before you go down that road, however, consider whether adopting an adult rabbit might be the better option for you. There are plenty of adult rabbits out there who have been abandoned by their previous owners and they are looking for a new forever home. When you adopt a rabbit you may actually save a life. Adopting a rabbit can sometimes be cheaper than buying from a breeder and, in many cases you get a cage and accessories with the adoption. Many adult rabbits ready for adoption have also already been spayed or neutered, litter trained, and they will be caught up on vaccinations.

Here is the list of breeders and adoption rescue websites around United States and United Kingdom:

Chapter Three: Purchasing Your Angora Rabbit

United States Breeders and Rescue Websites

Rabbit Breeders
<http://rabbitbreeders.us/angora-rabbit-breeders>

Rabbit Breeders (English Angora)
<http://rabbitbreeders.us/english-angora-rabbit-breeders>

Rabbit Breeders (Giant Angora)
<http://rabbitbreeders.us/giant-angora-rabbit-breeders>

National Angora Rabbit Breeders
<http://www.nationalangorarabbitbreeders.com/>

Evergreen Farm
<http://www.evergreenfarm.biz/about_us>

International Association of German Angora Rabbit Breeders
<http://iagarb.com/>

Bumble Bee Acres
<http://www.bumblebeeacres.com/EnglishAngoraBabyBunniesExpectedNewArrivals.htm>

Chapter Three: Purchasing Your Angora Rabbit

Exquisitely Angora Farms

<http://www.exquisitelyangora.com/Welcome.html>

Woolie Creations Angora Rabbits

<http://wooliecreations.net/>

Ocean Side Angoras

<http://www.oceansideangoras.com/>

American Rabbit Breeders Association

<http://www.arba.net/breeders.htm>

Class Act Angoras

<http://www.classactangoras.com/>

EwePorium

<http://eweporium.webs.com/angorabunnysforsale.htm>

Adopt – a – Pet

<http://www.adoptapet.com/s/rabbit-adoption>

Friends of Rabbits

<http://www.friendsofrabbits.org/info/adoption>

The Rabbit Haven

<https://therabbithaven.org/>

United Kingdom Breeders and Rescue Websites

Preloved UK
<http://www.preloved.co.uk/classifieds/pets/rabbits/all/uk/angora>

Rabbit Rehome
<http://www.rabbitrehome.org.uk/search/breed/angora>

British Rabbit Council
<http://www.thebrc.org/breeders-list.htm>

Bigwigs Angora UK
<http://www.bigwigsangora.co.uk/about-angora/>

Acomb Rabbit Rescue
<http://www.acombrabbitrescue.org.uk/>

British Giant Rabbits
<http://www.british-giantrabbits.co.uk/>

Pets 4 Homes UK
<https://www.pets4homes.co.uk/sale/rabbits/angora/>

Chapter Three: Purchasing Your Angora Rabbit

News Now UK

<http://www.newsnow.co.uk/classifieds/pets-animals/angora-rabbits-for-sale.html>

Selecting a Healthy Angora Rabbit

In the process of choosing a rabbit, make certain the Angora is in the pink of health and that it's living conditions are sanitary. Inquire about the kind of diet the rabbit has been fed and how it was reared and handled. Rabbits are most functional and mobile in the early hours of the morning and evening. Paying it a visit during that window period of day could reveal a better picture of the rabbit's temperament.

As potential Angora keeper, you have several sources where you can acquire an Angora rabbit. These include humane societies, pet shops, rescue organizations, and breeders. Questions you should ask yourself before selecting one should include answers of who will be the primary caregiver of the rabbit; the preferred size, color, and type of fur; and where the rabbit will be kept when taken home.

A healthy rabbit is to have well-groomed, shiny fur with no bald patches, scars or obvious wounds. Fur which is

Chapter Three: Purchasing Your Angora Rabbit

wet or matted, specifically around the chin or vent area, may be an indication of medical problems. There is to be no discharge from the Angoras eyes or nose, and no discharge or crusting in its ears. Rabbits which are healthy are typically alert and curious when active. They must not be hesitant to move about and is not to show any signs lameness or stiffness.

Chapter Three: Purchasing Your Angora Rabbit

Chapter Four: Caring for Your Angora Rabbit

At this point of your research, you will want to ask yourself if you are ready for a shift in your daily routine. Answer honestly when you ask yourself, if you will be able to pull away from a hectic lifestyle to care for your Angora and provide for its needs. You will need to figure out if this fuzzy faced bunny can fit the dynamics of your home. All pets rely heavily on their caregivers for their daily requirements and depend largely on the attention and care extended to them by dedicated and loving caregivers.

Chapter Four: Caring for Your Angora Rabbit

Whether the Angora is kept for wool production or if it is coming in as a pet addition to the family Angoras need a substantial amount of attention and care to thrive and live happily.

Habitat Requirements for Angora Rabbits

Rabbits have a higher chance of becoming better integrated as part of a family household if they are kept indoors. They are intelligent animals that can be trained to use a litter box and redirect natural tendencies, like gnawing at furniture and chewing on electrical wires, which are disruptive. Chewing on electrical wiring is hazardous for the rabbit and equally poses as a fire hazard. It can also become accustomed to being kept in an enclosure part of the time. Rabbits, when unsupervised, should be confined to safe quarters.

A rabbit hutch located in the basement, back yard, or garage is a popular housing location for rabbits. Diseases caused by neglect are commonly present in rabbits which were abandoned in a forgotten hutch. The rabbits' hutch must be easily accessible to responsible caregivers in order to provide proper care and attention to the rabbit. It should be adequately ventilated and protected from large dogs and other predators.

Chapter Four: Caring for Your Angora Rabbit

To give the rabbit's enclosure a homey feel, equip it with a watering system and a feed hopper it can run to when it gets a hankering for grub and glug. An empty, unfurnished cage is inadequate and boring; the environment of the rabbit's abode has to be furnished with toys and fitted with stimulating items that would engage and allow the rabbit to curiously explore whilst given something to engage in physically. Rabbits should optimally be given time outside of its cage for a necessary, daily romp around the yard.

Poor sanitation is the perfect breeding ground for diseases which cause illnesses and ultimately lead to death. It is therefore imperative that regular sanitation and a thorough cleaning of its digs be done. Nest boxes must be disinfected between uses and stored away for the next bout of kits. Cages, feeders, and watering system have to be sanitized periodically using an effective and inexpensive sanitizing solution.

Ideal Rabbit Cage

There are many, various kinds of hutches available at pet supply stores that can house an Angora rabbit. Of all available hutches at metal enclosure effectively avoids

Chapter Four: Caring for Your Angora Rabbit

unsanitary conditions, which can lead to health problems in the rabbit, because of its easy to clean surface.

The Angoras enclosure must be fashioned with 1-by-2-inch mesh on the sides and top and 0.5-by-1-inch mesh for the base. Planning on taking in more than one Angora rabbit? Hanging the enclosures from the ceiling rafters in single layers allows the keeper easier access and management.

Mature, adult bucks and does must have separate, individual enclosures which are at least 30 inches wide, 30 inches deep and 20 inches high. On the other hand junior does, fryers, and Angora rabbits - specifically the nonbreeding does and castrated bucks - can be housed together in small groups in one enclosure big enough to allow all ample moving space and territory.

Each enclosure must have a feed hopper as well as a watering system securely fastened on the outer part of the enclosure.

Chapter Four: Caring for Your Angora Rabbit

Indoor Cages vs. Outdoor Hutches

Angoras must be accommodated in an enclosure with a wire base, ideally, to allow its manure to fall through and not stick to its coat. A controlled climate environment is extremely favorable to an animal. However, most breeders choose to take cautious measures to prevent the rabbit from getting too warm or too cold during seasons of weather extremes.

Indoor cages, with a wire base, can be a haven of sorts for the Angora during the cold season, when the rabbit may find it unappealing to venture outdoors. This can also be utilized as its indoor enclosure on occasions when it joins the family for some homegrown R&R.

An outdoor hutch can be utilized during warmer seasons as long as the hutch does not trap heat within its walls. Outfit an outdoor hutch with proper lighting, ventilation and a blower which can help cool down the bunny during unusually warm days. Should this hutch be an option to allow the rabbit to stay outdoors during nighttime, make sure that the rabbit's habitat cannot be easily be broken into by tenacious, relentless predators.

Chapter Four: CARING for Your Angora Rabbit

Recommended Cage Accessories

The ideal floor space for the Angoras' enclosure should be big enough to allow the rabbit sufficient area mobility when it is in it. The caregiver is invited to use their imagination to think up novel accessories to furnish the rabbits enclosure. Here are a few ideas to throw in the pot; grab an old Slinky and cut it up to smaller slinky-tubes. Trace the rounded end of the Slinky on a piece of paper then cut out the cardboard circle and stick it on one end of a divided portion of the Slinky. Deposit a treat in the middle of the circle, hang up the Slinky and watch your rabbit go at it;

A block of hard, pesticide-free wood for the rabbit to gnaw on will not only engage your bunny, this will also help your Angora's teeth from growing too long; take an empty toilet roll carton and fold both its ends in toward the middle; do this by pushing down one side of the roll and then the other creating a flap. Repeat this for the other side. Before tying it up with some string, place a favorite toy of the rabbit inside. Push the cylindrical box around and in front of the rabbit to stimulate and whet its curiosity.

Chapter Four: Caring for Your Angora Rabbit

Litter Training Your Rabbit

The remarkable Angora rabbit is moderately trainable given a little time and patience. Litter training and rechanneling natural tendencies like chewing and digging are some basic "tricks" the keeper may want to teach the rabbit. Take time to understand what your rabbit maybe trying to tell you.

Since rabbits prefer relieving themselves in one place, litter training your Angora rabbit is as easy as it is possible at any age. Older rabbits have an advantage of being faster learners as compared to younger Angoras.

If a rabbit guardian gives the bunny the run of the house then litter training in a confined area is imperative. To do this, fill a litter box with organic litter and place some hay on top. Avoid using clay at all costs as this substance turns deadly should it find its way into the rabbits system and digestive tract. Set the litter box in one corner of a room or inside its enclosure. Put some of its own droppings into the litter box in an attempt to help the rabbit recognize the litter box as the place to do nature's business.

Chapter Four: Caring for Your Angora Rabbit

Handling and Taming Your Rabbit

The Turkish Angora rabbit is generally friendly and typically docile. It is an intelligent breed of Angora which has been a popular pet choice for many individuals and families alike.

This fuzzy fur-ball, if the caregiver chooses, is also a lucrative money-earner, due to its soft, long, silky wool which can be spun into yarn and be used to create shawls, blankets, throws, and even sweaters.

Your Angora rabbit does not and will not require you to carry it around. Excessive handling of the rabbit is discouraged to avoid accidental falling which can lead to injuries. Save handling the Angora for grooming periods when its wool needs its regular routine brushing.

Should its nails require trimming, you may limit its jerky movements by making a "bunny-burrito" of it - this is when the rabbit is swaddled loosely in a blanket to avoid injury to its fleshy paws. Speak softly and handle it with care to put it at ease.

Chapter Five: Meeting Your Rabbit's Nutritional Needs

The bulk of your rabbits' diet should largely consist of hay, grass, oat hay or timothy. Early introduction of certain fruits and herbs must gradually be introduced in the young rabbit's diet to help the animal acquire taste. Juvenile and adult rabbits must be given a balanced portion of dark leafy greens with a fresh hefty portion of hay or timothy. Serve this with its staple diet of pellets. You may sprinkle its food with sunflower seeds to aid the rabbit with digestion.

Chapter Five Meeting Your Rabbit's Nutritional Needs

Vegetables and fruits along with high-quality, high-fiber pellets should be diet staples for the growing rabbit and should be complemented with a very generous portion of grass, hay, or oat hay.

Look for the measure of fiber content in the pellet pills you feed your Angora. These should contain at least 13% fiber, not only allowing for better digestion but also to be rid of hairballs it may have swallowed whilst self-grooming.

Provide your rabbit an unlimited amount of fresh water because fecal impaction can be caused by dehydration which can absolutely be prevented. Give it water and lots of it. Encourage your Angora to drink more by providing it with a salt lick.

The Nutritional Needs of Rabbits

A healthy existence greatly hinges on the quality of food a living being ingests. A nutritionally sound diet suitable for the individual in question is an important foundation of health and well-being.

As with you and I, and no different from a pet cat or dog, the Angora rabbit's future wellbeing and overall good

Chapter Five Meeting Your Rabbit's Nutritional Needs

health is reliant on the quality of nutrition the Angora rabbit eats. A staple provision vital to keep the "flow of things moving" inside the Angora rabbit is good old hay. Hay is an important fiber production needed by the Angora to satisfy its daily fiber requirement.

Another staple that an Angora needs would be the unlimited supply of fresh water and lots of it. Rabbits require water at all times of the day and night. Lack of fresh water supply could lead to dehydration.

The furry-faced Angora thrives on a diet of high-quality food pellets. Depending on its mature weight, the Angora must be given a daily serving of 4-8 ounces of pellets. Mix in a heaping tablespoon of sunflower seeds to its feed. The seed's oil aids in the proper digestion of the rabbit as well.

The rabbit guardian may also feed the Angora green alfalfa sprouts. You may occasionally serve up a chunk of fruit with any seeds removed. A stick of carrot or a cut of sweet potato will also accepted by and are good for the Angora rabbit.

To keep your Angora happy an unlimited and abundant supply of hay, timothy, fresh grass, or oat hay should be provided. Hay provides and produces the fiber

Chapter Five Meeting Your Rabbit's Nutritional Needs

needed by the Angora to prevent dangerous wool block - also known as intestinal impaction.

Water is a necessary and regular need of the Angora and its keeper must not forget to set out a fresh bowl of H2O for the rabbit to drink from at any given time.

Toxic Foods to Avoid

Rabbits possess a sensitive digestive system which requires a special high fiber, low sugar and low fat diet. Here is a list of human foods that you must avoid feeding your rabbit:

- Avocado
- Beets
- Bread
- Chocolate
- Coffee
- Citrus peels
- Corn
- Fresh peas
- Grains
- Green beans
- Legumes
- Nuts
- Onions
- Potatoes
- Rice
- Rhubarb leaves
- Seeds
- Sugar

Chapter Five Meeting Your Rabbit's Nutritional Needs

There are also a variety of plants which are poisonous to your Angora. Whilst most wild rabbits instinctively avoid these plants, in your backyard and being confined to a small area, your pet rabbit may decide to have a taste anyway. Here is a selective list of toxic plants to avoid:

- All plants that grow from bulbs
- Arum lily (cuckoo point)
- Bindweed
- Bracken
- Convolvulus (bindweed)
- Deadly nightshade (belladonna)
- Delphinium (larkspur)
- Fools parsley
- Foxglove
- Apple (seeds)
- Apricot (all parts except fruit)
- Onion
- Tomato (leaves, vines) Tulip (bulb)
- Macadamia Nut
- Tomato Plant
- Most evergreens
- Poppies
- Wild Cucumbers
- Wild peas
- Potato tops
- Ragwort
- Wild Parsnip
- Rhubarb leaves
- Woody nightshade
- Wild Carrots
- Rhubarb Leaves
- Wild Carrots
- Almond

If your rabbit eats any of these foods, contact the Pet Poison Control hotline right away at (888) 426 – 4435.

Chapter Five Meeting Your Rabbit's Nutritional Needs

Tips for Feeding Angora Rabbits

Overfeeding is any rabbit's worst enemy. When a rabbit becomes overweight this condition of obesity can shorten the longevity of a rabbit and reproduction problems will become an issue alongside a host of other complications.

The amount of feed your rabbit consumes depends largely on the breed and size of the animal. Typically, smaller breeds can consume 3 - 5 ounces of feed each day, whilst larger breeds consume 6 - 10 ounces of food daily. Some rabbits shall need slightly more feed than those of the same breed, depending on their individual characteristics. You must determine the appropriate amount of food to feed your rabbit without overfeeding it. Supplements or treats can be given however; green leafy vegetables are NOT recommended (with exception of alfalfa hay).

Chapter Six: Breeding Your Angora Rabbit

Medium-weight breeds of 9 to 12 pounds are able to begin breeding between 6 to 7 months of age, with male rabbits maturing one month later than its female counterpart. Since outward indications of heat are not always obviously present in mature does, the caregiver must follow a strict schedule when breeding.

A single buck is able to service about 10 does but no more than two to three times a week. Put the female Angora in the buck's enclosure for breeding to happen.

Chapter Six: Breeding Your Angora Rabbit

Never bring the buck to the doe's enclosure as she will fight to protect her territory. Mating should happen immediately, and once done, the doe should then be returned to her enclosure.

The average period of gestation lasts 31 to 32 days. Twenty-eight days after a successful breeding, put the nest box in the doe's hutch and you will soon see a litter of kits grace the space.

An average commercial litter consists of 8 to 10 kits. Forty-eight hours after birth, the keeper should take note of and count the kits. Make sure that all kits are living and should any of the kits be unfortunate in continuing existence, remove its carcass from the litter immediately.

Take away the nest box from the doe's hutch 5 to 21 days after birth. The young rabbits will be weaned in about 30 days, so you should expect an average of five litters annually for every doe. With proper management, a good doe can continue to produce maximum-sized litters for 2 to 3 years.

A multitude of Angoras reared all at once are primarily kept and bred to produce wool. The harvesting, gathering and collection of Angora hairs requires a specific

Chapter Six: Breeding Your Angora Rabbit

skill set along with the application of long-standing harvest and collection techniques.

These efficient and historically time-tested techniques reached the pinnacle of specialization in France, back when it once held the prestige of being the pioneer producer and exporter of Angora wool across the world. Taking France's place is China, now in the throes of further developing this specialization.

Basic Rabbit Breeding Information

Medium to large sized rabbit breeds are sexually mature at 4 to 4.5 months, giant breeds at 6 to 9 months, and small breeds like the Dutch and the Polish Dwarf, at 3.5 to 4 months of age. The eggs released in female rabbits are set off by sexual intercourse and not by a cycle of hormones - like us humans. The rabbit has a receptive mating cycle. Meaning rabbits are receptive to the act of mating about 14 of every 16 days.

A doe is most receptive to mate when its vagina is red and moist. On the other hand, does that are not responsive to male courtship display a whitish pink vagina color with little or no moisture.

Chapter Six: Breeding Your Angora Rabbit

One technique to detect pregnancy in a doe is to feel the doe's abdomen for grape-sized embryos in the uterus. The right time to test for buns-in-the-oven is 12 days after breeding. False pregnancy is when the rabbit shows signs of pregnancy but is not pregnant, is quite common in rabbits.

Angora keepers and breeders strongly recommend the careful selection of breeding rabbits whose ancestry historically shows good productivity and good genetics. This is one time when productivity records and pedigrees listing show winnings come in handy. Keep a file of productivity and show records of your herd just for this purpose.

A female Angora pregnancy typically stretches out for about a month until the mother is ready to birth its baby bunnies which is around or about 31 to 33 days. Does with a small litter of four or less appear to have lengthier pregnancies than those that produce more litter.

If a doe has not given birth by the 32nd day of her pregnancy, your veterinarian will likely induce labor. Otherwise, a dead litter is almost always delivered sometime after day 34. There are occasions when a pregnant doe aborts or resorbs fetuses due to a disease or lack of nutrition.

Chapter Six: Breeding Your Angora Rabbit

Mating Behavior of Rabbits

Rabbits are active breeders and are well known to produce numerous quantities of kits in short periods of time. Due to this, busy active bunch, there are notable concerns of overpopulation with both wild and domestic rabbits all over the world. Because of this reality it is crucial that we find out the facts of the rabbit's mating habits and routine so as to gain a better awareness and understanding of when, and how often a rabbit reproduces.

The mating season of rabbits begin during the warm seasons to allow newborn baby bunnies in the wild the best chances of surviving. During the seasons of spring and summer, the amount of light available triggers an increase and release of hormones in rabbits which starts to change a rabbit's behavior. Male bucks will start to act more aggressively and frantically as hormones set of their sex drives. They will vie with the other male rabbits in the cage for the favors of the opposite sexed rabbits. Typically the more dominant rabbits are the more successful breeders at this competition and are commonly able to mate with more females.

Once a male buck has successfully won the attention of a female rabbit, the doe positions herself flat on the

Chapter Six: Breeding Your Angora Rabbit

ground and will start to lift up her tail. The buck then mounts her and bites down hard on her nape. The mating lasts about twenty seconds then the male releases the doe from bite grip and will lose consciousness, likely with a mouthful of fur.

Once pregnant with buns, the gestation period lasts about one month. The female will then give birth to anywhere from three to eight bunnies, all of which are blind and hairless. The female rabbit is able to and can birth a few times each year.

Nesting Requirements

The nesting box is to be placed inside the rabbit enclosure on the 28th day (3 days before scheduled kindling). Placing the nesting box any earlier will often result in losing a lot of the bedding because rabbit like to burrow or it uses the nesting box as a toilet.

Lay the box with soft hay and/or shavings of pine about 3 days before the doe is due to kiln. You may notice the doe pull hair out of her dewlap (the roll under her chin) and fashion a cozy bed for her young. The buns should come around somewhere between 28 to 31 days after a successful mating.

Chapter Six: Breeding Your Angora Rabbit

The doe shall be spending a lot of her time outside the nesting box and will only go back to feed the kits twice or so a day. The kits should be hopping in and out of the box often after about 3 weeks. The keeper can then safely remove the nesting box from the enclosure. Make sure that you clean and sanitize the nesting box for the next batch of kits. It is also advised to assign a nesting box to each doe exclusively to avoid possible cross-contamination.

Diet and Labor Process for Pregnant Angora Rabbits

The fact that Angora rabbits require specialized care and a specific diet in order for it to thrive well had been mentioned a few times earlier in this writing. This is true as well for farmed Angoras cared for and kept for breeding purposes.

The measure of time put into the Angora rabbit production labor can be subdivided into five categories:

- Food distribution
- Hair harvesting, gathering and collection
- Clean up and disinfection of enclosures, hutches, cages
- Preventive or curative health care (vaccinations)
- Reproduction

Chapter Six: Breeding Your Angora Rabbit

Distributing food or feeding the Angoras is not and need not be labor-intensive given that the breeder provides only high-quality balanced pellet feeds in feeders that are easily accessible.

To illustrate an example, 40 minutes per day and 210 hours per year will be spent by an Angora keeper to distribute food to a production unit of 400 Angora rabbits. Time is multiplied twice for the distribution of coarse feed such as cereals and hay. Factor in the daily transport, sifting of roughage or straw and the distribution of feed and this raises the time spent on feeding labor to 400 hours per year, inclusive of fasting days.

The process of harvesting, gathering up and the collection of hair is the most time-consuming operation. The calculation of labor time spent needs to include not only the actual removal hair by cutting, shearing, or plucking, to be reckoned in is the transport of the rabbit from its hutch to the collecting table. Following that the grooming phase to eliminate debris and/or vegetation matter from the coat should be added, after which, weighing the different grades of hair, documenting, placing the rabbit back into its hutch, and finally employing postharvest thermal stress reduction measures. Summing it up, about 1,000-hours per year are required for a production unit of 400-rabbits.

Chapter Six: Breeding Your Angora Rabbit

The time it takes for the complete removal and clear-out of soiled litter from hutches and wire-mesh enclosures must be taken into account. Add to this the length of time it takes to carry out disinfection procedures for each space. And finally, the amount of time it takes to sweep out the rabbit hutches and enclosures comes to a total of at least 250 hours of time spent on cleaning labor per year. Vet care is primarily a preventive measure; inoculations and general disease detection and prevention can take up to 175 hours of time spent on vet visits per year.

Tasks related to reproduction such as the handling of breeding animals, checking gestation and kindling, sexing newborn rabbits, and weaning would also require 175 hours per year spent on general jobs related to reproduction. In all, a production unit of 400 Angora rabbits would require an Angora keeper to toil 2,000 working hours per year under normal production conditions.

Raising Baby Rabbits

Angora kits are birthed naked, blind, and deaf. They then start to display hair a few days after birth. The eyes and ears open on day 10. Rabbits as newborns are not capable of regulating their body temperatures until about the 7th day. Rebreeding can happen any time after giving birth. People

Chapter Six: Breeding Your Angora Rabbit

who raise rabbits for show or as pets like to rebreed 35 to 42 days after the birth of a litter.

Almost all medium to large-sized female rabbits possess 8 to 10 nipples, and a lot of them give birth to 12 or more kits. Should a doe be unable to effectively nurse all the kits, those kits may be fostered by giving them to a doe of about the same age with a smaller litter within the first 3 days after kindling. Should the fostered kits be mixed up with the foster doe's own kits and covered with hair of the fostering doe, they are commonly accepted by the rest. Migrating larger kits to the new litter, and not the smaller kits, increases the chance of success. Kits would nurse for less than 3 minutes at a time and does nurse only 1 to 2 times every day. Kits wean about 4 to 5 weeks of age.

Newborn must be kept warm, dry, and be in a quiet environment. Substitute doe's milk for a formula of ½ cup evaporated milk, ½ cup water, 1 egg yolk, and 1 tablespoon corn syrup can be used. Feeding ratio varies from ½ teaspoon to 2 tablespoons, depending on the age of the kits or uses a kitten milk replacer. Kits start eating greens around day 15 to 18. It is possible to raise kits by hand.

Young does sometimes kill and eat their young for a number of reasons like failure to nurse and nutritional deficiency. Predators, like dogs, enter a rabbitry often and

Chapter Six: Breeding Your Angora Rabbit

cause nervous mother does to kill and eat the young. Cannibalism of dead kits occurs as a natural, nest-cleaning instinct. Should a keeper be attentive to all proper management practices and the doe continues to kill 2 litters in succession, she should not be used for breeding.

Chapter Six: Breeding Your Angora Rabbit

Chapter Seven: Grooming Your Angora Rabbit

These furry bunnies are typically calm and can be handled with ease. Its amiable nature works to the advantage of the keeper because the Angora will require frequent and regular grooming to tame its long, luscious locks and maintain the natural shimmer of its coat. Begin grooming and regular, routine handling of your Angora whilst the rabbit is young. In this way it gets used to the repeated procedure and gives little to no resistance in future grooming sessions.

Chapter Seven: Grooming Your Angora Rabbits

If left alone and not combed out the Angoras wool will mat and tangle. Forcing out the tangles will be painful for the rabbit and you may have to resort to the untimely shearing of its wool. If you see loose tendrils of falling wool, this is your cue to step up on the grooming schedule.

Another reason for the keeper to carry out this task dutifully is that Angoras groom themselves similar to what felines do and they tend to swallow loose hair. When cats do this, they are usually able to cough up the hairball. This is not so for rabbits, hence, any hair it swallows stays lodged inside them. When this occurs, it is called "wool block".

Wool block prevents the rabbits from eating properly because they have the false sensation of being full. This can lead to starvation and if prolonged, death. To avoid this situation from occurring feed your rabbit lots of fiber in the form of hay. There is also a bounty of rabbit food rich in fiber available in pet supply stores. To help things move along, always set out lots of water for it to drink.

Recommended Tools to Have on Hand

The most important tool when grooming your Angora is YOU. As the guardian and keeper of this amusingly fuzzy rabbit, whose face seems lost in a sea of

Chapter Seven: Grooming Your Angora Rabbits

wool, your dedication to the task, understanding for the need to carry out the job and religiously carrying out the necessary chore is key to the daily coat care of your furry Angora.

Rabbits whose wool becomes matted are in for gravely serious health issues. Ingestion of wool will cause the rabbit to eat less and if left unnoticed and untreated, this could lead to its demise by starvation. It will be difficult to resist that teeny face lost in an ocean of long, shiny fur anyway, so you can look forward to some much needed quality downtime with your agreeable buddy.

Whether the Angora you acquire is pet or wool producer what you will need is a wide-toothed comb and a slicker brush. If you are playing with the idea of showing your Angora rabbit, you will also require a high-speed blower. Blowers do not come cheap but it is going to be a required tool if Angora showing turns out to be an acquired hobby later on.

Chapter Seven: Grooming Your Angora Rabbits

Tips for Bathing and Grooming Angora Rabbits

Before attempting to groom your Angora make sure you have all the necessary tools within your reach. You and your rabbit will be there for a while - 30 to 40 minutes for non-shedding periods and 40 to 60 minutes during weeks of profuse shedding - so have a bowl of green treats to offer your Angora should it begin to fidget and become restless.

Thank your lucky stars for the amicable demeanor of the Angora rabbit. This easy-going trait of it will work for you during grooming sessions. You may experiment by placing the rabbit on a waist-high table whilst resting it on a non-slip pad. Most Angora guardians have found that placing the rabbit on a blanket laid out on your lap not only catches the falling wool, the blanket also serves as a gentle security restraint.

Place the rabbit on your lap and face it away from your body. Take a handful of the rabbit's wool and firmly but gently pull the wool straight up.

Now with your other hand use the slicker brush to take hold of the base of the grasped coat of wool. Pick up a small amount of wool and proceed to brush the wool away from the Angoras body.

Chapter Seven: Grooming Your Angora Rabbits

Repeat this action making sure to grab a little more wool than the first time. Keep repeating this making sure the rabbit is rotated into positions that will keep it agreeable and calm.

For areas where a bit of matting is apparent, employ the wide-toothed comb to gently loosen the tangles then go over the area with the slicker brush.

Pay keen attention to the chin area of the Angora, between its ears as well as the long hairs on the sides of its cheeks. Side "furnishings" are the long hairs on the face and head of the Angora. Unkempt furnishings will become matted because if the rabbit eats out of crocks or earthenware bowls.

Time to pay careful mind to the Angora rabbits abdomen. This is the area that picks up debris the most and is more prone to matting than the rest of its body. Whilst holding its ears and the scruff of its neck, gently, but firmly, turn the rabbit on its back. Its legs should not

Position the rabbit's ears between your knees, careful not to pinch them. Calmly speaking to it in hushed tones, begin to brush the stomach area of the Angora a little bit at a time just as you did with its top body.

Chapter Seven: Grooming Your Angora Rabbits

Be mindful of this position when you lean in over your rabbit as it could use its powerful back legs to deliver a swift, powerful kick if spooked or hurt. Avoid getting scratched by staying alert.

For areas that have hopeless matting and felting your only recourse is to snip off the area. Do this with great care as the Angoras skin is thin and will easily cut. You can use grooming scissors with blunt, rounded out ends to avoid accidental injuries.

So long as the rabbit is groomed regularly, debris routinely removed from its wool and its fur free of matting and felting, bathing is not necessary. However, if it is absolutely necessary, localize the areas that need washing. Use a non-medicated shampoo meant for cats and dogs. Use a hypoallergenic shampoo that has conditioners. Avoid using made-for human shampoo as this will dry out the luscious coat of your Angora.

Rabbits are not fond of water so keep the water warm to provide some soothing comfort to the rabbit. Slowly lower the rabbit into the warm, shallow water and proceed to quickly lather its wool. Rinse its coat thoroughly with a mild stream of warm water.

Immediately wrap the rabbit in a warm towel and remove as much excess water as possible before training a blow dryer on its body. Use a warm setting and never turn up the setting to high heat.

Other Grooming Tasks

As with brushing and grooming your Angoras wool, so should you pay mind to its nails. You may carry out this job whilst the rabbit is on its back. Make sure that its hind legs are pointed away from your face and body.

Gently push aside the fluff of the feet and with the aid of a small pair of nail clippers, trim the tip of the nail. White nails are easier to locate and see but if the nails of your rabbit are dark it can be more challenging to spot the quick of its nail.

Proceed with caution and be careful not to cut too far into the quick as nicking it will result in profuse bleeding. Should this happen apply direct pressure to the nick using a clean paper towel for a good minute or so, and then dip the nail in styptic powder to help the blood clot. A pinch of cornstarch is a good alternative for styptic powder.

Chapter Seven: Grooming Your Angora Rabbits

Chapter Eight: Showing Angora Rabbits

The American Rabbit Breeders Association has specific guidelines and standards for Angora keepers to follow should they want to have their Angora participate at a show. Read on to find out what these specifications are and this should help Angora aficionados prepare for a spectacular display.

Chapter Eight: Showing Your Angora Rabbits

Angora Rabbit Breed Standards

English Angora

Let us begin with the only breed of Angora with facial furnishings - the English Angora. This typically gentle and sweet natured Angora has a rich, thick coat which needs daily, intensive grooming to avoid matting and tangling. This breed should display a compact body and it is to resemble a round fluffy ball when posed. There should be dense wool on the rabbits head as well as the sides of its head.

Its cranium must be broad as well as flat across the rabbit's nostrils. The English Angoras ears are to show short and fringed or tasseled abundantly.

The English Angoras coat is characterized by having tiny guard hairs in proportion to its wool. Its coat should have a healthy, silky texture, should wrap tightly when spun with minimal fluffing and must be fall few. There is to be a good distribution of guard hair and must be evident to assist in the support of the crimped under wool. The wool of the Angora must not part over the back and fall to the sides giving it a flat appearance.

Chapter Eight: Showing Your Angora Rabbits

The junior doe and junior buck must weigh a minimum of 2 3/4 pounds. The junior doe must not weigh over 6 pounds and the junior buck shouldn't weigh over 5 1/2 pounds. The minimum weight for a senior buck and a senior doe is 5 pounds.

A senior doe is not to weigh more than 7 1/2 pounds and a senior buck should not weigh more than 7 pounds. The ideal weigh for both senior buck and doe is 6 to 6 1/2 pounds.

When the English Angora is judged, the majority of points are based on its wool. These criteria include wool density, length and texture. Points for the "General Type" include its body type, the head, its ears, eyes, feet, legs and tail.

French Angora

The French Angora has no wool furnishings on its head, ears, face or front feet. Its ears may be plain or they may be tufted, with the tufting restricted to its ear ends. Its cranium must be oval in shape and is to be balanced with the size and shape of its physique. The head must also have trimmings on the sides. When viewed from its profile, the French Angora should have an oval-shaped appearance. When viewed down it should have an oblong shape.

Chapter Eight: Showing Your Angora Rabbits

The French Angora wool should have an abundance of guard hairs which must protrude above the under wool. There must be a good balance of guard hair and under wool. The under wool should be heavily crimped. Its wool must be vibrant, fall free and strong.

The junior buck and doe should not weigh over 7 1/2 pounds. Its minimum weight should be 3 3/4 pounds. Both junior buck and doe can weigh between 7 1/2 to 10 1/2 pounds with an ideal weight of 8 1/2 pounds.

When judging the French Angora, majority of points are based on its wool including thickness, texture and length. The "General Type" points include its body physique, its head, ears, eyes, feet, legs and tail.

Giant Angora

The sole 6-Class animal in the breed is the Giant Angora. This rabbit should display a commercial type physique with a thick, dense coat of wool. Its head is to be oval and must be broad across the forehead, slightly narrower toward the muzzle. Its forehead shall have tufts or head trimmings and cheek furnishings. The trimmings on its head are to be noticeable. The head trimming of the doe is not as heavy as that on the buck. Its ears are to be lightly fringed and tasseled.

Chapter Eight: Showing Your Angora Rabbits

This is the only breed of Angora which is solely shown as ruby-eyed white. The coat of the Giant Angora has three fiber kinds to give it texture. Its under wool should be the dominant hair over the other two types of hair. It must be medium fine, delicately waved, soft and must have a gentle shine. Its awn fluff is to have a guard hair tip and is wavy, stronger wool. The awn fluff is located between the awn hair and under wool. The awn hair, alternately known as guard hair, is the third sort of hair fiber. The awn hair is strong and straight which protrudes above the wool and should be evident and present.

The Giant Angora is classified differently than the three other Angora breeds because it is a 6-Class animal. Both junior buck and doe should be below 6 months of age and must weigh a minimum of 4 3/4 pounds. Both buck and doe of intermediate range are to be 6-8 months of age. Both senior buck and doe should be 8 months or over in age. The senior buck should weigh 9 1/2 pounds at least. The senior doe should weigh 10 pounds at least.

When judging Giant Angoras, majority of points are based on its wool, including thickness and density, texture, and length. Points for "General Type" include the body type, its head, its ears, eyes, feet, legs and its tail.

Chapter Eight: Showing Your Angora Rabbits

Satin Angora

The body of the Satin Angora is to be of medium length with good width and depth. Its sides must have a slight taper beginning at the hindquarters all the way to its shoulders. Its head is to be oval. Its forehead should be broad and narrow at the muzzle. Its head must be balanced with the rest of its body. Its ears should be plain or a tad tufted; however tufting should be limited to the tips of its ears.

The Satin Angoras wool is much finer than the wool of the rest of the Angora breeds. The wool of the Satin Angora should be fine, soft and silky. There should be a crimp in its under wool. Its wool should be shiny and must display sheen. The comparatively smaller diameter and transparency of the hair shaft gives a reflective light which provides the hair richness in color. Its coats sheen should be obvious over the whole body from its nose to its tail.

Both junior doe and junior buck should not weigh over 6 1/2 pounds and must weigh a minimum of 3 3/4 pounds. Both senior doe and senior buck can weigh from 6 1/2 to 9 1/2 pounds. The ideal weight for a Satin Angora is 8 pounds.

Chapter Eight: Showing Your Angora Rabbits

The Satin Angora carries the most points amongst all Angora breeds on its wool including density, thickness, sheen, texture and length. Points for "General Type" include its body type, its head, its ears and eyes, its feet and legs as well as its tail.

Preparing Your Rabbit for Show

After making sure that your Angora rabbit is an excellent specimen of the breed, you can start thinking about entering a show. The first thing you need to do is become a member of whatever organization you hope to show your rabbit with – this will likely be either the ARBA or the BRC. Once you have become a member you will be able to register your rabbit under your name and enter him in shows. It can sometimes take a little while to complete this process so stay up to date with shows in your area so you can enter your rabbit as soon as your registration is completed.

When you are ready to enter your rabbit into a show, start by reading the rules and regulations for that specific show. In most cases, registering your rabbit for a show is fairly easy but you want to make sure you don't overlook anything that might get you disqualified. Make sure you adhere to the deadlines for registration and have all of the information you are likely to need handy.

Chapter Eight: Showing Your Angora Rabbits

Here is the information needed to compete:

- Your name and address
- The breed of your rabbit
- Your rabbit's color and age
- The sex of your rabbit
- Whether you bred or transferred the rabbit
- Whether you are a juvenile exhibitor

Once you have registered your rabbit all that is left is to wait until the show day. Prior to the day of show, make sure that you know how to get there and make sure you have a copy of the schedule so you know exactly when your rabbit is shown. In the days leading up to the show you should put together a kit of items that may come in handy on show day. Also keep in mind the following things needed:

- Your registration information
- Food and water for your rabbit
- Nail clippers – for emergency nail trimming
- Hydrogen peroxide – for cleaning injuries and spots on white coats
- Slicker brush and other grooming supplies
- Business cards, contact information
- Paper towels and wet wipes
- Scrap carpet square – for last-minute grooming
- Collapsible stool – when chairs are not available

Chapter Eight: Showing Your Angora Rabbits

- Extra clothes, food, and water for self

On the day of the show, plan to arrive at the venue at least 30 minutes prior to judging, and then proceed to your assigned pen. At this point, the best thing to do is to sit back and watch – you can learn a lot just by observing at a rabbit show. When it comes time for judging, all you can really do is wait and let the judges do their duties. Your rabbit must remain in his pen for the duration of the judging. If you rabbit wins anything, a prize card will be placed on his pen. When the judging is over, you can take your prize cards to the secretary and collect your prize money.

At this time, you can feel free to leave the show or you can stick around to keep learning. Take advantage of this opportunity to connect with other rabbit owners – you never know what you might learn or how a new connection could benefit you.

Chapter Eight: Showing Your Angora Rabbits

Chapter Nine: Keeping Your Rabbit Healthy

Just as a responsible and dedicated keeper would care for a cat or dog, so should they care for their pet Angora rabbit. Your Angora will certainly need periodic visits to the vet throughout the year and this is a good time to make sure that all is on the up and up with its health.

The Angora rabbit is prone to a number of diseases and may fall ill sooner or later whilst under your care. It is up to you, as its caregiver, to find out about which illnesses it can be susceptible to and - should one manifest - how to handle medical situations as it occurs and whilst en route to your trusted vet.

Common Health Problems Affecting Rabbits

Rabbits are prone to several diseases such as myxamatosis, tularemia, pasteurellosis, coccidiosis, enterotoxemia, encehpalitozoonosis and RHD. In this section, you'll learn what these diseases are and how you can prevent it from affecting your pet.

Tularemia is a zoonosis which is frequently contracted when wild rabbits are hunted for purposes of game.

Myxamatosis was once utilized by Australia to contain the population of wild rabbits. As time passed these rabbits developed immunity to the disease.

RHD is presently used to control the pest rabbit population in Australia and New Zealand (Fenner and Fantini, 1999). It was in 2000 when the Rabbit Hemorrhagic Disease (RHD) was first seen in the U.S. RHD can potentially affect both the commercial and pet rabbit populations in the U.S.

Chapter Nine: Keeping Your Rabbit Healthy

Pasteurellosis is a common reason of respiratory disease in rabbits. When a rabbit becomes exposed to this, it harbors the organism which causes this illness and if it develops, this can potentially develop as a chronic disease which is hard to contain or control.

Primarily affecting young, weaned rabbits between six weeks to five months of age, Intestinal Coccidiosis is attributed to noise, stress, transportation or immunosupression. The symptoms of this illness, if present in the Angora rabbit, usually manifests within four to six days after infection. Signs of illness include a rough coat, dullness, dehydration, decreased appetite and weight loss.

Enterotoxemia is a severe diarrhea which your rabbit may experience. This commonly seen in rabbits 4-8 weeks old but can affect rabbits at any age. Diets lacking in fiber content can be a cause of this illness. If the rabbit is not equipped to handle stress, this can be a reaction to the stress it experiences. Transitioning to a new environment or being around new people (strangers) can also cause the symptoms to arise. Incorrect intake of antibiotics is also a usual culprit of this very sudden, very messy stomach condition.

Encephalitozoon cuniculi is an intracellular, obligate, microsporidian parasite typically seen in pet rabbits.

Chapter Nine: Keeping Your Rabbit Healthy

Ingestion is the most common method of transmission. E. cuniculi has a predilection for the kidneys and brain. Neurologic signs caused by E. cuniculi often include torticollis, nystagmus, ataxia, or rolling. Other neurologic signs may include seizures, urinary incontinence, a stiff rear gait, and posterior paresis. Should the keeper suspect their rabbit to suffer from this, immediately bring the Angora rabbit to the vet to begin treatment.

Error! Bookmark not defined.Preventing Illness

In the U.S. rabbits are dual-purposed animals raised as family pets for some, and a source of meat for others. It is imperative for any responsible rabbit keeper to determine what they can do to avoid rabbit illness. Awareness on what can be done to keep your pet rabbit healthy is a job for the rabbit's caregiver. To maintain a healthy rabbit other important factors to remember and employ are, to provide it good ventilation, to employ keen observation, to ensure its protection from the elements and above all to maintain cleanliness of pet habitat.

Rabbits can succumb to a number of diseases which can endanger its health and life. Pasturella multocida is the culprit of a decrease in rabbit productivity and a staggering mortality rate in does.

Chapter Nine: Keeping Your Rabbit Healthy

It is advised to restrict casual visitors who may carry the disease, infect and cause stress to the rabbit. It is also strongly recommended to keep children in the room.

Should you, the caregiver, observe and notice an injured or sick rabbit, immediately isolate the animal until you have nursed it back to health. Disinfect both the regular enclosure and isolation cage of the animal to avoid the spread of diseases.

Keep a record on each animal (if you have more than one in your care) for a good health program to be effective. Provide tattoo identification for each rabbit with breeding and health information attached to its hutch.

Recommended Vaccinations

Vaccinating is a very touchy topic and can ruffle some people's feathers with the mere mention of the word. As with any conflicting information, specially the medical kind, it would be best to consult with your veterinarian about which avenue to take.

Ideally a vaccine against the deadly Calicivirus protects your rabbit against this highly contagious malady which is spread by fleas and mosquitoes.

Chapter Nine: Keeping Your Rabbit Healthy

At 10 - 12 weeks of the Angoras life is its first inoculation followed by the second one four weeks after the first vaccine was administered. A booster shot is scheduled annually after it has been given its second vaccine. Beginning at eight weeks deworms your rabbit once every three months thereafter.

Signs of Possible Illnesses

All pets have their weaknesses and susceptibility to illnesses. As previously mentioned, a keepers keen observation is vital to the continued health of the rabbit.

If your pet Angora suffers from diarrhea, if you notice an increase in appetite but is accompanied by weight loss, if it has a dull coat, pale gums, scaling skin, lethargy, irritability, self-biting or behavioral traits out of the ordinary may signal the rabbit to be ill.

Rabbit Care Sheet

You've made it until the end! You are now on your way to becoming a very well-informed and pro-active Angora rabbit owner! Finishing this book is a huge milestone for you and your future or present pet, but before this ultimate guide comes to a conclusion, keep in mind the most important things you have acquired through reading this book. This chapter will outline the summary of what you have learned, including the checklist you need to keep in mind to ensure the wellness of your Angora rabbit.

Basic Information

Pedigree: domestic rabbit; medium to large size breed

Group: the British Rabbit Council (BRC), American Rabbit Breeders Association (ARBA).

Breed Size: Medium, large and long depending on breed

Weight:

Male/Female:
English Angora: 2.0–3.5 kg (4.4–7.7 pounds)
French Angora: 3.5–4.5 kg (7.7–9.9 pounds)
Satin Angora: 3.0–4.5 kg (6.6–9.9 pounds)
Giant Angora: 5.5 kg or larger

Coat Length: long coat

Coat Texture: fine, fluffy

Color: Ruby-Eyed White, Blue-Eyed White, Tortoiseshell, Seal, Sable, Red, Pointed White, Opal, Lynx, Lilac, Fawn, Copper, Chocolate, Chinchilla, Chestnut, Blue, and Black.

Mane: Single or Double

Temperament: docile, gentle, friendly, active

Strangers: may be wary or scared around strangers

Other Rabbits: generally good with other rabbit breeds if properly trained and socialized.

Rabbit Care Sheet

Other Pets: friendly with other pets but if not properly introduce may result to potential aggression

Training: intelligent, responsive and very trainable

Exercise Needs: provide toys for mental and physical stimulation

Health Conditions: generally healthy but predisposed to common illnesses such as myxamatosis, tularemia, pasteurellosis, coccidiosis, enterotoxemia, encehpalitozoonosis and RHD

Lifespan: average 7 to 12 years

Habitat Requirements

Ideal Habitat: free-run in the home with some kind of shelter or large cage with opportunities to exercise.

Cage Requirements: large enough for rabbit to move freely, easy to clean, safe.

Minimum Cage Size: at least 4 to 6 times the length of the rabbit when stretched out

Ideal Cage Size: 24 x 36 x48 or an XL size

Exercise Requirements: at least everyday

Rabbit Care Sheet

Indoor vs. Outdoor: outdoor has more space, easier to clean, less noise and odor; indoor is safer, better for human interaction, and easier to monitor

Cage Accessories: water bottle, food bowl, hay rack, litter pan, nest box/shelter, toys

Recommended Bedding: meadow hay, timothy hay, natural fiber blanket

Bedding to Avoid: straw, shredded newspaper or cardboard, wood shavings, pine or cedar

Litter Training: place litter tray in the area your rabbit habitually uses to relieve himself

Recommended Litter: fresh hay lined with newspaper

Litter to Avoid: cat litter, clumping litter, scented litter, dusty litter

Nutritional Needs

Diet Type: herbivore

Nutrition Basics: low protein, high fiber

Dietary Staples: high-quality commercial pellets, grass hay, oat hay, fresh vegetables, fresh fruits

Pellets: at least 18% fiber, purchase no more than 6 weeks' worth at a time to keep fresh

Rabbit Care Sheet

Hay: alfalfa hay is okay for babies; timothy hay and other grass hays are a staple; supplement with oat hay

Vegetables: leafy greens should make up 75% of fresh diet; feed about 1 to 2 cups per 6 pounds of bodyweight daily

Fruit: no more than 1 to 2 ounces per 6 pounds of bodyweight daily

Water: unlimited access to fresh water at all times

Baby Rabbits: Substitute doe's milk for a formula of ½ cup evaporated milk, ½ cup water, 1 egg yolk, and 1 tablespoon corn syrup can be used. Feeding ratio varies from ½ teaspoon to 2 tablespoons, depending on the age of the kits or uses a kitten milk replacer. Kits start eating greens around day 15 to 18. It is possible to raise kits by hand.

Young Adults: increase timothy hay, grass hay, and oat hay; decrease alfalfa hay; decrease pellets to ½ cup per 6 pounds bodyweight; increase vegetables and fruits

Mature Adults: unlimited timothy hay, grass hay, and oat hay; ¼ to ½ cup pellets per 6 pounds bodyweight; minimum 2 cups vegetables per 6 pounds bodyweight; ration no more than 2 oz. fruit per 6 pounds bodyweight daily

Senior Rabbits: maintain adult diet as long as healthy weight is stable; add alfalfa hay or increase pellet consumption for underweight rabbits

Rabbit Care Sheet

Breeding Information

Sexual Maturity (female): average 6 to 7 months old

Sexual Maturity (male): average 6 to 7 months old

Breeding Age (female): around 9 months to 1 year

Breeding Age (male): around 6 months

Breeding Type: multiple cycles per year, continuous

Mating Protocol: add the doe to the buck's cage; rebreed at least one for better chance of success

Palpation: should be able to feel marble-sized embryos after about 2 weeks since mating

Litter Size: average of 8 to 10 kits

Gestation Period: around 31 to 32 days

Nesting Box: minimum requirement is about 24 x 30 x36

Bedding: soft straw, haw, or pine shavings; mother will add some of her own fur

Characteristics at Birth: eyes and ears closed, little to no fur, completely dependent on mother

Fur Development: 5 to 6 days

Eyes Open: 10 to 12 days

Begin Weaning: around 4 weeks; does will reduce milk production after 3 weeks

Rabbit Care Sheet

Index

A

accessories 33
adopt 33
age 5, 80
alfalfa 92, 93
American Rabbit Breeders Association 3
angora 3
Animal Welfare Act 106
APHIS 106
appearance 3
ARBA 3, 79

B

baby 5, 7, 33
back 6, 81
bedding 107
belly 5
birth 5, 6
birthing 5
blood 6
body 4, 6
bodyweight 93
box 5, 6, 92
BRC 4, 79
breed 33, 79, 80, 94
breeding 5, 33
breeds 3, 4, 33
British Rabbit Council 4, 106
broken 4
brush 80
buck 94

C

cage	33, 91, 94
care	105, 107
characteristics	3
chin	4
cleaning	80
coat	3, 4, 5, 6, 7, 90
coloring	3
condition	6

D

diet	93, 107
doe	5, 94

E

ears	3, 94
embryos	94
exercise	91

F

female	4, 93
fiber	92
food	4, 6, 7, 81, 92
fruit	93
fur	3, 4, 6, 7, 94

G

genes	6
grooming	4, 80
guard hairs	3, 4, 6, 7

H

hair 3, 6
hay 92, 93
head 3
healthy 93

I

intact 4
intelligent 91

J

judging 81

K

kindling 5, 94
kits 5, 6
kittens 94

L

leafy greens 93
legs 4, 6, 7
litter 4, 33, 92, 106
loin 6

M

male 4, 6, 93, 94
marking 3
meat 5
milk 6, 93, 94

N

nails 6
nest 5, 6, 92
noise 7, 91
nutrition 4

O

offspring 4, 6
organization 3, 79
outdoor 91

P

pattern 6
pellets 92, 93
Pet Poison Control 52
pet store 33
pets 90
pregnant 5, 6
prize 81
protein 92
purchase 92

R

regulations 79

S

scent 4
schedule 80
self 81
selling 4
shedding 6
shoulders 3

show 79, 80, 81
skin 3
solid 7
spayed 33

T

teeth 6
texture 6
time 5, 81, 92
timothy hay 92
type 3

U

unaltered 4
undercoat 3, 4, 5, 6

V

vegetables 92, 93

W

water 80, 81, 92, 93
water bottle 92
weight 93

Photo Credits

Page 1 Photo by user wildlifeartbykaz via Pixabay.com, https://pixabay.com/en/rabbit-grass-spring-bunny-green-2230208/

Page 2 Photo by user Neko412 via Pixabay.com, https://pixabay.com/en/rabbit-angora-rabbit-japanese-rabbit-1296926/

Page 19 Photo by user Jannes Pockele via Flickr.com, https://www.flickr.com/photos/jpockele/2106513328/

Page 30 Photo by user Emily Neef via Flickr.com, https://www.flickr.com/photos/darkmoonslayer/5858626419/

Page 39 Photo by user Jannes Pockele via Flickr.com, https://www.flickr.com/photos/jpockele/2105735755/

Page 48 Photo by user Dennis Harper via Flickr.com, https://www.flickr.com/photos/dennisharper/5798584401/

Page 54 Photo by user vjmarisphotos via Flickr.com, https://www.flickr.com/photos/purduepics/8067286849/

Page 65 Photo by user Zoomed In via Flickr.com, https://www.flickr.com/photos/zoomed-in/3869136283/

Page 73 Photo by user vjmarisphotos via Flickr.com, https://www.flickr.com/photos/purduepics/15737343953/

Page 83 Photo by user vigilant20 via Flickr.com, https://www.flickr.com/photos/lynnszwalkiewicz/4802022097/

Page 89 Photo by user Lanafactum via Wikimedia Commons, https://commons.wikimedia.org/wiki/File:White_Satin_Angora_Rabbit.jpg

References

All Rabbit Breeds by Alphabetical Order - RabbitBreeds.org
http://www.rabbitbreeds.org/all-rabbit-breeds-c-g.php

Angora Rabbit - Raising – Rabbits.com
http://www.raising-rabbits.com/angora-rabbit.html

Angora Rabbit - RoysFarm.com
http://www.roysfarm.com/angora-rabbit/

Angora Rabbit - American Rabbit Breeders Association
http://www.arba.net/

Angora Rabbit Breeds – National Angora Rabbit Breeders
http://nationalangorarabbitbreeders.com/angora-rabbit-breeds.htm

Angora – Rabbits Facts - Petcha.com
https://www.petcha.com/angora-rabbits-facts/

A Beginner's Guide to Angora Rabbit Care – Maine Angora Producers
http://www.maineangoraproducers.com/begin_guide.html

Breeding Rabbits - Debmark.com
http://www.debmark.com/rabbits/breeding.htm

Breeding and Reproduction of Rabbits – Merck Veterinary Manual
http://www.merckvetmanual.com/all-other-pets/rabbits/breeding-and-reproduction-of-rabbits

Choosing Your Pet Rabbit - House Rabbit Resource Network
http://rabbitresource.org/care-and-health/you-and-your-rabbit/choosing-your-pet-rabbit>

Cleaning Rabbit Cages - Rabbit Breeders
<http://rabbitbreeders.us/cleaning-rabbit-cages>

Coccidiosos in Rabbits - Nutrecanada.com
www.nutrecocanada.com/docs/shur-gain---specialty/coccidiosis-in-rabbits.pdf

Enterotoxemia – Vetary.com
https://www.vetary.com/rabbit/condition/enterotoxemia

Facts on Rabbits – Peta.org
https://www.peta.org/issues/companion-animal-issues/companion-animals-factsheets/facts-rabbits/

Going to Shows - The British Rabbit Council
http://www.thebrc.org/going-to-shows.htm

Housing and Companionship for Your Rabbits
Blue Cross for Pets
https://www.bluecross.org.uk/pet-advice/housing-and-companionship-your-rabbits

How to Bathe an Angora Rabbit - ehow.com
http://www.ehow.com/how_8582443_bathe-angora-rabbit.html

How to Groom Angora Rabbits - The Cape Coop
http://www.thecapecoop.com/how-to-groom-angora-rabbits/

Licensing and Registration under the Animal Welfare Act APHIS
https://www.aphis.usda.gov/animal_welfare/downloads/aw/awlicreg.pdf

Litter Training - House Rabbit Society
http://rabbit.org/faq-litter-training-2/

Nestboxes - AZRabbits.com
http://www.azrabbits.com/useful-information/nestboxes.html

Pasteurella in Rabbits – Long Beach Animal Hospital
www.lbah.com/word/rabbit/pasteurella-rabbit/

Rabbit Bedding - Just Rabbits
http://www.justrabbits. com/rabbit bedding.html#gs.sqfNHnk

Rabbits by Body Type - Mosaic Rabbitry
http://mosaicrabbitry.weebly.com/rabbits-by-body-type.html

Rabbit Care - Essendon Veterinary Clinic.
http://essendonvet.com.au/pet-library/rabbit-care

Rabbit Food - House Rabbit Society
http://rabbit.org/faq-diet/

Rabbit Info – Save A Fluff UK
https://www.saveafluff.co.uk/

Rabbit Mating Habits - EzineArticles.com
http://ezinearticles.com/?Rabbit-Mating-Habits&id=2812428

Rabbit Mating – Raising – Rabbits.com
http://www.raising-rabbits.com/rabbit-mating.html

Rabbit Nutrition - Vet Secure
https://www.vetsecure.com/animalmedcen.com/articles/29

Rabbit Production - PSU.edu
http://extension.psu.edu/business/ag-alternatives/livestock/additional-livestock-options/rabbit-production

Rabbit Vaccinations, Desexing, Worming and More - Petstock.com
https://www.petstock.com.au/petcare/rabbit-care/vaccinations-desexing-worming-more#

Rabbit Terms – Terminology Words Used in Rabbitry - Just Rabbits
http://www.justrabbits.com/rabbit-terms.html

Useful Info - Rabbit Rescue Canada
http://rabbitrescue.ca/

Want to Foster a Rabbit? - Friends of Rabbits
http://www.friendsofrabbits.org/

Feeding Baby
Cynthia Cherry
978-1941070000

Axolotl
Lolly Brown
978-0989658430

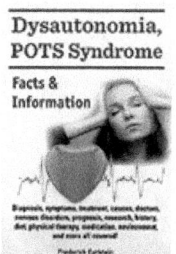

Dysautonomia, POTS Syndrome
Frederick Earlstein
978-0989658485

Degenerative Disc Disease Explained
Frederick Earlstein
978-0989658485

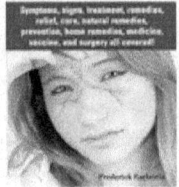

Sinusitis, Hay Fever,
Allergic Rhinitis Explained
Frederick Earlstein
978-1941070024

Wicca
Riley Star
978-1941070130

Zombie Apocalypse
Rex Cutty
978-1941070154

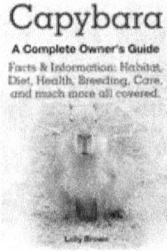

Capybara
Lolly Brown
978-1941070062

Eels As Pets
Lolly Brown
978-1941070167

Scabies and Lice Explained
Frederick Earlstein
978-1941070017

Saltwater Fish As Pets
Lolly Brown
978-0989658461

Torticollis Explained
Frederick Earlstein
978-1941070055

Kennel Cough
Lolly Brown
978-0989658409

Physiotherapist, Physical Therapist
Christopher Wright
978-0989658492

Rats, Mice, and Dormice As Pets
Lolly Brown
978-1941070079

Wallaby and Wallaroo Care
Lolly Brown
978-1941070031

Bodybuilding Supplements
Explained
Jon Shelton
978-1941070239

Demonology
Riley Star
978-19401070314

Pigeon Racing
Lolly Brown
978-1941070307

Dwarf Hamster
Lolly Brown
978-1941070390

Cryptozoology
Rex Cutty
978-1941070406

Eye Strain
Frederick Earlstein
978-1941070369

Inez The Miniature Elephant
Asher Ray
978-1941070353

Vampire Apocalypse
Rex Cutty
978-1941070321

www.ingramcontent.com/pod-product-compliance
Lightning Source LLC
LaVergne TN
LVHW051645080426
835511LV00016B/2498